...to you but sorry,
...mixed up so do...
...thing straightened
...going to let me
...just cannot settle
...thing, haven't even
...hay left to do...
...lonesome—it seem...
...uldn't stand it,...
...now that's foolish...
...get over yet but no...
...said ... A. M.—the...
...sick storm...
...am all through...

To:

_____

From:

_____

Mom's Prayer Journal
Copyright © 2004 by Fern Nichols
ISBN 0-310-80983-5

Requests for information should be addressed to:
Inspirio, the gift group of Zondervan
Grand Rapids, Michigan 49530
http://www.inspiriogifts.com

Published in association with the literary agency of Ann Spangler & Associates, 1420 Pontiac Rd. SE, Grand Rapids, Michigan 49506

Compiler: Molly C. Detweiler
Project Manager: Tom Dean
Design Manager: Val Buick
Design: Gayle Raymer
Handwriting image: csaimages.com

Printed in China
04 05 06/HK/ 4 3 2 1

A Guided Journal by
Fern Nichols

Mom's PRAYER JOURNAL

inspirio™

Dear Friends,

I am so thankful that many years ago I was encouraged to keep a prayer journal for my children. Now I have the awesome privilege of going back to those pages and seeing how God has faithfully worked in their lives and answered so many prayers.

God revealed himself to me as I praised him in writing. He made me more like his Son, Jesus, through my confessions. He gave me a grateful, joyful heart through my thanksgiving for answered prayer. He taught me to ask with confidence according to his will in my intercessions. He continues to teach me to pray. And I continue to journal.

There is no greater legacy I can leave my children and grandchildren than the legacy of my prayers. Long after I am gone, my prayers will continue to be an enduring part of God's touch on their lives. My journals hold my treasures of the goodness of God—legacies of prayer that will last forever.

You too can leave a personal legacy to your children, even in the midst of the busy seasons of motherhood. Planning is the key to the success of a regular quiet time. Pick a place where you can go each day with your Bible, a pen, and your prayer journal. Even if you can only get away for 10 or 15 minutes, God will use that time to refresh and inspire you.

As you begin, ask God to quiet your heart and open your eyes so you may see the wonder and peace in his Word. Do your best to set aside all those issues that might distract you from your time with him.

In your quiet time with God, you will be guided progressively through the sections of Praise, Confession, Thanksgiving, and Intercession. Each of the steps will help you to reflect on a different aspect of God's character. Open your heart and pour out your love, hopes, dreams, and faith onto these pages.

Praise

Begin your quiet time with praise. The Holy Spirit will speak to your heart with wonderful thoughts about who God is. Write those thoughts down by penning a simple prayer of praise. Our prayer life is shaped on how well we know God, grow closer to him, and build our personal relationship with him. "Be still, and know that I am God" (Psalm 46:10).

Confession

Pray this prayer before you confess your sin: *"Search me, O God, and know my heart; test me and know my anxious thoughts. See if there is any offensive way in me, and lead me in the way everlasting"* (Psalm 139:23–24).

Thanksgiving

A heart of gratitude will emerge as you obey the Word of God. *"Be joyful always; pray continually; give thanks in all circumstances, for this is God's will for you in Christ Jesus"* (1 Thessalonians 5:17–18). Recording God's answers to your prayer requests will help you to remember his faithfulness to meet all your physical, spiritual, and emotional needs.

Intercession

This is a time to pour out your heart before the Lord for the life of your child. You will tap into the power of God as you believe the promise: *"Let us draw near to God with a sincere heart in full assurance of faith. ... Let us hold unswervingly to the hope we profess, for he who promised is faithful"* (Hebrews 10:22–23). God will hear and answer your prayers.

My prayer is that this journal will help you grow closer to Jesus and provide a once-in-a-lifetime treasure of prayer for your own children.

Fern Nichols

– FOUNDER OF MOMS IN TOUCH INTERNATIONAL

God is Love

Dear Father, I ask you to forgive me for the times I have doubted your love. Please forgive me when I withhold your love from others and wound their spirits. I am sorry. Thank you for forgiving me.

God is Love

Loving Father, thank you for loving my child regardless of what he has done or will do. Thank you for your unchanging love that knows no boundaries. I am so grateful that you are always reaching out with your saving love.

Thanksgiving

_____

_____

_____

_____

_____

_____

_____

_____

_____

_____

_____

_____

_____

_____

_____

intercession

God is Love

Lord, I ask that my child will experience your unconditional love. I pray he will know how deep and wide, how strong and enduring is your personal love for him. May he find his greatest joy and fulfillment in your love. Help him to see that your love is changeless and eternal.

God is Forgiving

Is it difficult to forgive yourself for things you have done?
Let God's forgiveness sink down deep into your soul,
healing you once and for all.

Whoever confesses ... finds mercy.

PROVERBS 28:13

confession

_____

_____

_____

_____

_____

_____

_____

_____

_____

_____

_____

_____

_____

_____

_____

_____

_____

thanksgiving

God is Forgiving

As high as the heavens are above the earth,
so great is God's love for those who fear him,
as far as the east is from the west,
so far has he removed our transgressions from us.

PSALM 103:11–12

_____

_____

_____

_____

_____

_____

_____

_____

_____

_____

_____

_____

_____

God is Forgiving

Pray for your child to accept God's forgiveness through his Son, Jesus (Romans 3:22–24). Pray your child is able to humble herself and ask for forgiveness (Psalm 149:4).

intercession

God is Good

Who is a God like you,
*   who pardons sin and forgives the transgression*
*   of the remnant of his inheritance?*
You do not stay angry forever
*   but delight to show mercy.*

Micah 7:18

_____

_____

_____

_____

_____

_____

_____

_____

_____

_____

_____

_____

_____

God is Good

Quiet your heart and consider God's goodness to you and your family, friends, church, home, and children. Give thanks for each one and the goodness of the Lord.

thanksgiving

_____

_____

_____

_____

_____

_____

_____

_____

_____

_____

_____

_____

_____

_____

_____

_____

God is Good

intercession

My God, I pray my child believes that you are good and a refuge in times of trouble. May my child believe your promise that no matter what the problem is, even the ones she creates herself, will work out for her best good. May her heart once again be joyful.

praise

God Hears

*The eyes of the LORD are on the righteous
and his ears are attentive to their cry.*

PSALM 34:15

_____

_____

_____

_____

_____

_____

_____

_____

_____

_____

_____

_____

_____

_____

_____

_____

God Hears

confession

Dear Lord, I confess to you those times that I deliberately disobey and turn away from you, allowing my pride to surface and dictate my actions. Afterward I feel guilty and ashamed and wonder how you could forgive me again. Forgive me for trusting my feelings and doubting your promises that you will hear and forgive me.

God Hears

Be still and give joyous thanks for this truth:

In my distress I called to the LORD;
    I cried to my God for help.
From his temple he heard my voice;
    my cry came before him, into his ears.

PSALM 18:6

_____

_____

_____

_____

_____

_____

_____

_____

_____

_____

_____

_____

_____

_____

_____

_____

_____

_____

_____

_____

_____

_____

_____

_____

_____

_____

_____

_____

_____

God Hears

Dear Father, I ask that you place in my child's heart a strong belief in your promise that as your child, he can approach you with confidence. May he know that if he asks anything according to your will, you hear and will give him whatever he asks of you.

intercession

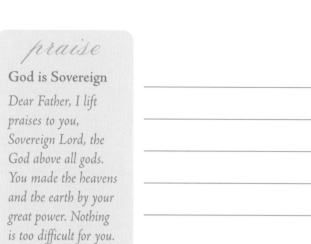

praise

God is Sovereign

Dear Father, I lift praises to you, Sovereign Lord, the God above all gods. You made the heavens and the earth by your great power. Nothing is too difficult for you. There is none like you.

_____

_____

_____

_____

_____

_____

_____

_____

_____

_____

_____

_____

_____

_____

_____

God is Sovereign

confession

Forgive me for being fretful and fearful instead of trusting.
My Father, in the midst of unknowns I want to trust in
your sovereign, loving plan for my child's life and not be afraid.

_____

_____

_____

_____

_____

_____

_____

_____

_____

_____

_____

_____

_____

_____

_____

_____

_____

_____

God is Sovereign

Thank God for the difference it makes in your life when you trust in his sovereign plan for you. Rejoice that there is nothing that can touch you or your children outside the will of God.

thanksgiving

God is Sovereign

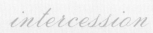

*Pray for your child to know that God will work
all things together for the good of those who love him
(Romans 8:28). Ask God to reveal to your child
that he cares about the smallest details in her life
(Matthew 10:29–31).*

God is Faithful

O LORD God Almighty, who is like you?
You are mighty, O LORD, and your faithfulness surrounds you.

PSALM 89:8

_____

_____

_____

_____

_____

_____

_____

_____

_____

_____

_____

_____

_____

_____

_____

God is Faithful

confession

In quietness and trust is your confidence. Ask the Holy Spirit to search your heart and open it to receiving God's promises of love and encouragement. Experience the truth of God's faithful promise that he will forgive you so you can be supportive of your child.

God is Faithful

Father, I am filled with loving gratitude for the promise that your mercies are new every morning. I start each new day knowing your blessings are available to me all day long. No matter where life takes me, your mercies are more than adequate to meet each need.

thanksgiving

_____

_____

_____

_____

_____

_____

_____

_____

_____

_____

_____

_____

_____

_____

_____

_____

_____

_____

_____

_____

_____

_____

_____

_____

_____

_____

_____

_____

_____

_____

_____

God is Faithful

intercession

*Dear Father, I ask you to be a shield around my child,
be his glory and the lifter of his head. Please come
alongside of him through the power of your Holy Spirit
and change his "I cannot" to "I can."*

God is Righteous

Dear Forgiving Father, I confess that I get caught up in the pursuit of things that do not reflect your righteousness. Fill me with your Holy Spirit and empower me to be a godly woman. May all that I do bring you glory.

_____

_____

_____

_____

_____

_____

_____

_____

_____

_____

_____

_____

_____

_____

_____

God is Righteous

Meditate on what it means that Christ's righteousness became yours when you accepted him into your heart. Thank God for every wonderful detail and circumstance of your salvation.

thanksgiving

_____

_____

_____

_____

_____

_____

_____

_____

_____

_____

_____

_____

_____

_____

_____

_____

_____

_____

_____

_____

_____

_____

_____

_____

_____

_____

_____

_____

_____

_____

_____

intercession

God is Righteous

Pray your child will seek the Lord first (Matthew 6:33).
Pray for your child to grow in the grace and knowledge of Jesus (2 Peter 3:18).
Ask God to lead your child into his light (Ephesians 5: 8–10).

God is My Strength

I love you, O Lord, my strength. I marvel at your strength that I see in your creation, in your deliverance, and even in the light of my human weakness. I praise you for the promise that you will give strength to those who ask for it.

confession

God is My Strength

Dear Lord, I admit that I am trying to handle things myself. Forgive me for relying on myself. Help me to remain in you and rely on your strength to do right.

God is My Strength

thanksgiving

Whom have I in heaven but you?
    And earth has nothing I desire besides you.
My flesh and my heart may fail,
    but God is the strength of my heart
    and my portion forever.

PSALM 73:25–26

_____

_____

_____

_____

_____

_____

_____

_____

_____

_____

_____

_____

_____

intercession

God is My Strength

*God's Promise for Your Child: Your child can do
everything through Christ who gives him strength.*

PHILIPPIANS 4:13, AUTHOR'S PARAPHRASE

_____

_____

_____

_____

_____

_____

_____

_____

_____

_____

_____

_____

God is My Teacher

This is what the LORD says—
your Redeemer, the Holy One of Israel:
"I am the LORD your God,
who teaches you what is best for you,
who directs you in the way you should go."

Isaiah 48:17

praise

God is My Teacher

Dear Lord, I admit that I have not always been willing to learn. I have often ignored your guidance and have missed opportunities to teach my children your life-changing commands. Please forgive me. Please help me to listen to you and be open to receiving the lessons only you can teach.

_____

_____

_____

_____

_____

_____

_____

_____

_____

_____

_____

_____

_____

_____

God is My Teacher

My Lord, thank you for teaching me your ways so that I will be fully instructed to follow in obedience. Your patience as a teacher is always personal, gracious, and kind. I trust you to help me teach my children.

thanksgiving

God is My Teacher

Father, I pray you will teach my child your way, because you are her God. I ask that the Holy Spirit would lead her on level ground. May your words always ring true in her mind. I pray the Holy Spirit will guide her into all truth.

_____

_____

_____

_____

_____

_____

_____

_____

_____

_____

_____

_____

_____

_____

_____

_____

_____

God is My Helper

My help comes from the LORD,
the Maker of heaven and earth.

PSALM 121:2

praise

God is My Helper

Are you struggling with particular situations or people in your life? Have you asked God for his help and guidance? Is there something preventing you from asking for God's help? Tell the Lord of your struggles, and he will hear your cry for help.

_____

_____

_____

_____

_____

_____

_____

_____

_____

_____

_____

_____

_____

_____

_____

_____

_____

_____

_____

_____

God is My Helper

Dear Caring Father, thank you for coming to my aid every time I seek your help and for always responding to me with loving-kindness. I rejoice that with your help I have the strength and resolve to tackle hard situations and make progress.

thanksgiving

God is My Helper

Pray your child will ask God for his wisdom
(Jeremiah 33:3).
Pray that your child will work with all his heart to please
God (Colossians 3:23).
Pray that his teachers will be encouraging
(1 Thessalonians 5:14).

_____

_____

_____

_____

_____

_____

_____

_____

_____

_____

_____

_____

_____

_____

_____

_____

_____

_____

_____

_____

_____

_____

_____

_____

_____

_____

_____

_____

_____

God is Able

Dear Father, there are many times I feel inadequate. I often complain that I don't have the personal qualities necessary to do specific tasks, so I procrastinate, despair, or give up. You are able to make all grace abound to me for everything that I need to be successful.

confession

God is Able

Give thanks by reflecting on the fact that there is nothing God cannot do.
God can give you guidance when you have no idea what to do.
God can provide for your child's needs in answer to your prayers.
He is able to give courage in the face of fear.

_____

_____

_____

_____

_____

_____

_____

_____

_____

_____

_____

_____

_____

_____

_____

_____

_____

God is Able

Dear Gracious Father, I ask that your grace will abound to my child. My child doubts her talents and abilities. She feels incapable and lacks confidence. I pray for your grace to be on her life so that she will excel in the abilities that you have given her.

intercession

God is Wise

Dear Lord, what security I have in knowing that you are God of all wisdom. I praise your power and unlimited ability to discern and judge what is true and right. I marvel at the depth of your wisdom and knowledge.

_____

_____

_____

_____

_____

_____

_____

_____

_____

_____

_____

_____

_____

_____

_____

_____

_____

confession

God is Wise

How are you using your time? Search your heart and think about what is important to God. There is a time and a place for everything. With God's wisdom and guidance, you will find the answers.

God is Wise

Dear All-Wise God, I thank you for each new day. Your ways are perfect; you cannot make a mistake. In your infinite wisdom you have ordained each day of my life. I anticipate my tomorrows with wonder.

thanksgiving

God is Wise

*Pray that your child seeks the Lord's face always
(1 Chronicles 16:11). Pray that she becomes wise through
the Word (Psalm 19:7–8; Matthew 7:24). Pray that
your child will be filled with the knowledge of God's will
(Colossians 1:9).*

Jesus is the Bread of Life

Are there sins in your life that are preventing you from being physically and spiritually healthy? Name them and give them to Jesus; he is strong. Feel the weight of the burden lifted from your shoulders to his. Feel his peace.

Jesus is the Bread of Life

thanksgiving

Dear Jesus, I am forever grateful for the Bible. I love the Scripture. It is the source of everything that I need to grow in spiritual strength and wisdom. Thank you for the times your words have brought me hope and sustained me when I was crushed in my spirit.

_____

_____

_____

_____

_____

_____

_____

_____

_____

Jesus is the Bread of Life

Gracious Father, I pray that my child will trust in you with all her heart and lean not on her own understanding, but acknowledge you in all her ways, and you will make her paths straight.

intercession

praise

God is the Creator

Creator God, you alone are the Maker of heaven and earth. You are the one who brought the universe and all life into existence. By your word you spoke all things into being out of nothing. The heavens and the earth declare your glory; blessed be your glorious name.

_____

_____

_____

_____

_____

_____

_____

_____

_____

_____

_____

_____

_____

_____

God is the Creator

Dear Lord, forgive me for criticizing the way you made me. How many times have I wanted to change my appearance and not appreciated that you created me to be just the way I am? Help me to become as beautiful on the inside as I want to be on the outside.

_____

_____

_____

_____

_____

_____

_____

_____

_____

God is the Creator

Read all of Psalm 139 whenever you feel down and tempted to question how you look. Read it again to remind yourself that you are fearfully and wonderfully made. Thank God for his attentive care over all he has made.

thanksgiving

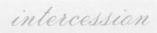

God is the Creator

My Father, you created my child's inmost being; you knit him together in my womb. May he praise you because he is fearfully and wonderfully made; may he believe that your works are wonderful. O Father, help him to know that you do not make mistakes, that he was uniquely designed by you.

God is the Great Physician

My Great Physician, I praise you as the source of all healing. You heal all manner of diseases and sicknesses. As the Lord who heals, you have shown yourself to be compassionate, caring, and full of mercy. How great is your love that you heal and make whole.

_____

_____

_____

_____

_____

_____

_____

_____

_____

_____

_____

_____

_____

_____

God is the Great Physician

Dear Great Physician, my child is sick and I am growing weary in faith and physical stamina. Father, I don't want my child to feel like he is a burden to me. Help me to be patient and loving, and forgive me when I doubt your wisdom and power to heal.

confession

God is the Great Physician

thanksgiving

"When you pass through the waters,
    I will be with you;
and when you pass through the rivers,
    they will not sweep over you.
When you walk through the fire,
    you will not be burned;
    the flames will not set you ablaze.
For I am the LORD, your God,
    the Holy One of Israel, your Savior."

ISAIAH 43:2–3

_____

_____

_____

_____

_____

_____

_____

_____

_____

_____

_____

_____

_____

_____

_____

_____

_____

_____

_____

_____

_____

_____

_____

_____

_____

_____

_____

God is the Great Physician

Pray for God's healing power and that your child does not lose heart (2 Corinthians 4:16). Ask God to help your child learn to comfort others with the same comfort he has received from God (2 Corinthians 1:3–4).

intercession

God is My Stronghold

Lord, with delight I acknowledge that you are my stronghold—your very presence is my protection. The storms of life will come, but I am safe within impenetrable walls.

_____

_____

_____

_____

_____

_____

_____

_____

_____

_____

_____

_____

_____

_____

_____

_____

God is My Stronghold

Do you experience regret when you run from the stronghold of God's protection? What areas of your life do you try to cover up? Do not forget, guilt is gone when you confess your sin.

confession

_____

_____

_____

_____

_____

_____

_____

_____

God is My Stronghold

God my Stronghold, I thank you for the personal protection that you give my children and me. You are a mighty fortress, a strong tower, whose walls cannot be penetrated or destroyed. No enemy can touch my children or me when we are safe within your arms.

thanksgiving

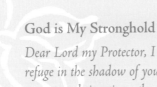

God is My Stronghold

intercession

Dear Lord my Protector, I pray that my child will take refuge in the shadow of your wings. You know the circumstances and situations, the places and people that cause my child to feel at risk. I trust you, Lord, to meet my child and protect her.

Jesus is the Beloved

Loving Lord, my heart seems far from your love. I have neglected the reading of your Word and prayer causing me to feel far from you. Forgive me for allowing the distance between us. I so crave your warm embrace of love.

Jesus is the Beloved

Dear Father, I am overwhelmed with gratitude to be called beloved just as you call Jesus beloved. It makes me feel so special to know that you wanted me. There is absolutely no greater realization than knowing I am your beloved child.

thanksgiving

_____

_____

_____

_____

_____

_____

_____

_____

_____

_____

_____

_____

_____

_____

Jesus is the Beloved   *intercession*

*Dear Gracious Father, I ask that my child will know that
by your grace, she has been accepted in Jesus, your beloved
Son. Lord, it tears my heart apart to see my child deal
with feeling rejected, insecure, and unloved. Please show
your unfailing love to her.*

Jesus is My Friend

Do you have friendships that need to be restored?
Are you holding a grudge? Feel the cleansing of the
Holy Spirit as you obey his voice.

Jesus is My Friend

In what ways has Jesus been a friend to you? Reflect on the many ways he shows you his friendship and how that makes you feel. How does that make you feel?

thanksgiving

_____

_____

_____

_____

_____

_____

_____

_____

_____

_____

_____

_____

_____

_____

_____

intercession

Jesus is My Friend

Pray your child's love for his best friend, Jesus, grows deep (Ephesians 3:16–19).

Ask God to help your child to know the value of friends (Ecclesiastes 4:9–10).

Pray for your child to be a forgiving friend (Proverbs 17:9).

Ask God to help your child be a witness to her unsaved friends (1 Peter 3:15).

God is Gracious

Dear Lord, I confess my bitterness and retaliation toward one who has hurt me deeply. I admit I have not extended the same forgiveness that you give me every time I sin. You immediately forgive and don't hold ill thoughts toward me. I want my relationship with you and with others to be right.

_____

_____

_____

_____

_____

_____

_____

_____

_____

_____

_____

_____

_____

_____

intercession

God is Gracious

Gracious Father, I pray for my child to be kind and compassionate to others, forgiving them just as God forgave her. She has been deeply hurt and is holding a grudge. I ask you to replace the spirit of bitterness with the spirit of forgiveness. May she experience the fruit of forgiveness.

The Fatherhood of God

Dear God, how very special is the fatherhood of God—it is of great value and significance. I praise you that as your offspring, I have the privilege of being under your authority and have access to your unlimited wisdom and boundless love.

The Fatherhood of God

*What are the influences that cause you to wander away
from God's direction and guidance? Trust God to help you
do better in the future. Anticipate the peace, security, and
happiness that will come as a result of obedience.*

_____

_____

_____

_____

_____

_____

_____

_____

_____

_____

_____

_____

The Fatherhood of God

thanksgiving

Father, I love the thought of you as my father and shepherd. I thank you for the image given in Isaiah of you gathering your children, young and old, in your arms and holding them close. I especially thank you for those times when I feel tired and weary and you carry me right where I can nestle close to your heart.

The Fatherhood of God

*Ask God to help your child understand the blessings of
honoring her parents (Colossians 3:20).*

*Pray that your child will listen and learn from you
(Proverbs 1:8–9).*

*Pray for your child to show proper respect to everyone
(1 Peter 2:17).*

God is Victorious

Dear Almighty God, I praise you that victory belongs to you. From your sovereign throne the view is always victorious, for you are the ultimate Victor. Nothing can stand against you. I praise you for you are my God of eternal triumph.

God is Victorious

Dear Lord, I am so disappointed and frustrated when I do those things that I know displease you. I lose my joy and feel defeated. I am sorry for my selfishness and pride. Fill me with your Holy Spirit and help me keep a pure heart.

_____

_____

_____

_____

_____

_____

_____

_____

_____

_____

_____

_____

thanksgiving

God is Victorious

Dear Heavenly Father, because Jesus overcame the world, I can too. Jesus said, "In this world you will have trouble. But take heart! I have overcome the world" (John 16:33). Thank you for your promise that the power of the Living Christ within me has given me victory over sin and temptation.

praise

God is My Heavenly Father

Heavenly Father, I exalt your name— you are my Father and I praise you. "Father" is the attribute that speaks of a close and intimate relationship. What a honor it is for me to call you Father. As your daughter, I rejoice in your infinite love.

_____

_____

_____

_____

_____

_____

_____

_____

_____

_____

_____

_____

_____

God is My Heavenly Father

confession

*Ask God, your Father, to show you where you are
following man-made thoughts and traditions rather than
God. Commit to studying God's Word so you can tell
the difference. Read Psalm 103:17–18 and hear God's
promise of love for you when you obey his precepts.*

_____

_____

_____

_____

_____

_____

_____

_____

_____

_____

_____

_____

_____

God is My Heavenly Father

My God, I am so thankful that you are my Father. I am abundantly blessed by all the fatherly things that you do for me. You are a Father I can count on, a Father I can trust. I love you.

thanksgiving

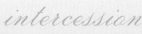

intercession

God is My Heavenly Father

My precious Lord, I pray that my child will choose earthly role models who reflect your nature. May she pledge allegiance to you, her Lord and Savior, and take pride in being called your child. I pray that you will always be her number one role model.

Jesus is a Servant

praise

*Lord, even as the Sovereign God you became a servant.
You descended from the highest heaven, where you reigned
in majesty and indescribable glory, to become human, Jesus
Christ. I adore you for leaving the splendor of heaven to
take on man's limitations and ultimate poverty.*

_____

_____

_____

_____

_____

_____

_____

_____

_____

_____

_____

_____

_____

_____

_____

_____

_____

_____

_____

_____

_____

_____

_____

_____

_____

_____

_____

_____

_____

_____

_____

_____

_____

_____

_____

_____

_____

_____

_____

_____

Jesus is a Servant

Thank you, Lord, for living a servant's life, caring and ministering to all those who needed your help. You turned no one away. How can I give adequate thanks for this marvelous demonstration of servanthood?

thanksgiving

_____

_____

_____

_____

_____

_____

_____

_____

_____

Jesus is a Servant

Lord, help my child use the gifts you have so generously given him to serve others. I ask that my child is sensitive to those around him. I pray that he will learn to honor others above himself.

praise

God is Ever-Present

Almighty God, I give you praise. There is no place that you are not. I am awestruck by the truth that your Presence encompasses all space. You always see me, always know what is going on in my life, and are always there as my constant resource of courage and strength.

_____

_____

_____

_____

_____

_____

_____

_____

_____

_____

_____

_____

_____

confession

God is Ever-Present

My Ever-Present God, I want to be totally devoted to you but am swayed by the emotions of the moment. Please help me to remember all the difficulties you have brought me through and draw courage from your power and promise to always be with me.

thanksgiving

God is Ever-Present

Where can I go from your Spirit?
  Where can I flee from your presence?
If I go up to the heavens, you are there;
  if I make my bed in the depths, you are there.
If I rise on the wings of the dawn,
  if I settle on the far side of the sea,
even there your hand will guide me,
  your right hand will hold me fast.

PSALM 139:7–10

_____

_____

_____

_____

_____

_____

_____

_____

_____

_____

_____

_____

_____

_____

_____

_____

intercession

God is Ever-Present

Father, I pray for my child to be strong and courageous, unafraid and encouraged. Let her know that the Lord her God is with her wherever she goes. Please bless my child with a spirit of faith, for you have not given her a spirit of fear but of power, love, and a sound mind (2 Timothy 1:7).

_____

_____

_____

_____

_____

_____

_____

_____

_____

_____

_____

_____

_____

_____

_____

_____

_____

praise

God is Patient

You, O LORD, are a compassionate and gracious God,
slow to anger, abounding in love and faithfulness.

PSALM 86:15

God is Patient

My Merciful Lord, forgive me for my impatience. I can get so irritated with those I love the most. When I think about your patience with me, the offenses of others seem so small and insignificant.

God is Patient

Dear Jesus, I am truly thankful for your unlimited patience. I am thankful for your patience during the times I choose to exclude you from my life. Even then you are always waiting patiently for me to return.

thanksgiving

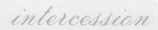

God is Patient

Dear Faithful God, may my child be strengthened with all power, great endurance, and patience according to your glorious might. May he wait patiently, trusting your promises. Please give him a heart that perseveres.

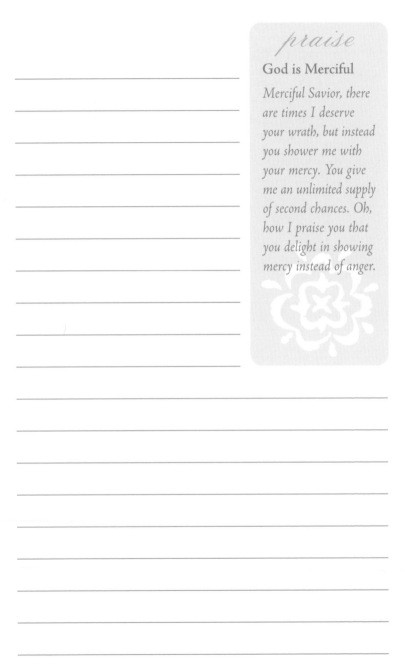

praise

God is Merciful

Merciful Savior, there are times I deserve your wrath, but instead you shower me with your mercy. You give me an unlimited supply of second chances. Oh, how I praise you that you delight in showing mercy instead of anger.

_____

_____

_____

_____

_____

_____

_____

_____

_____

_____

_____

_____

_____

_____

_____

confession

God is Merciful

*As you open your heart to the Holy Spirit's gaze,
what is he revealing? Words and actions that may
have wounded others? Continue in an attitude of
repentance, letting the Lord guide you as you pray.*

_____

_____

_____

_____

_____

_____

_____

_____

_____

_____

God is Merciful

Dear Father, I come with an offering of thanksgiving because of your tender expressions of mercy and love. I thank you that as your words sink deep into my heart, I will be a conduit of your mercy, kindness, and love.

thanksgiving

God is Merciful

Loving, Merciful Father, please help my child to not harbor anger, but be quick to resolve his conflicts so bitterness does not take root in his heart. Fill him with your wisdom so he is able to handle challenging situations in a loving and kind manner.

God is My Comforter

Dear Lord, I am going through a very painful time. I feel alone and uncomforted. I have accused you of not caring, of being absent from my life. I know deep in my heart this is not true. Wash away my tears and enable me by faith to feel the comfort of your arms wrapped tightly around me.

God is My Comforter

thanksgiving

Give thanks for God's promises of comfort:
when discouraged (Lamentations 3:20-23; Romans 8:28)
when weary (Matthew 11:28–30; Philippians 4:12–13)
when lonely (Isaiah 49:14–16; John 14:15–21)
when anxious (Matthew 6:25–27; Philippians 4:4–7)

_____

_____

_____

_____

_____

_____

_____

_____

_____

_____

_____

_____

_____

_____

_____

_____

_____

_____

_____

_____

_____

_____

_____

_____

_____

_____

_____

_____

God is My Comforter *intercession*

My Father, I ask you to bind up my child's broken heart. Please grant him a crown of beauty instead of ashes, the oil of gladness instead of mourning, and a garment of praise instead of a spirit of despair. My heart aches to see my child hurt and frustrated. I can't fix this. I wish I could. Only you, Jesus, can heal him.

_____

_____

_____

_____

_____

_____

_____

_____

_____

_____

_____

_____

_____

_____

_____

_____

_____

_____

God is Compassionate

praise

Almighty King, I worship you for being a God of infinite, matchless compassion. You empathize with and enter into our suffering, and bring healing and wholeness. Your compassion is like a mother having compassion on her children—you have a gracious heart, full of mercy and forgiveness.

God is Compassionate

Dear Lord, forgive me for the times I ignore my family's hurts. Help me to stop, listen, and tenderly care for my family with a compassionate heart. May compassion begin in my own home.

_____

_____

_____

_____

_____

_____

_____

_____

_____

_____

_____

_____

_____

_____

_____

_____

_____

God is Compassionate

Thank God for the ways in which you have personally benefited from Jesus' compassion. What has he delivered you from? Helped you through? Comforted you in? Expect his compassion today.

thanksgiving

God is Compassionate

Dear Jesus, I pray for my child to be clothed with compassion, kindness, humility, gentleness, and patience. May he seize opportunities to be caring and kind to others. Motivate him toward compassionate actions that will make a difference in his little corner of the world.

_____

_____

_____

_____

_____

_____

_____

_____

_____

_____

_____

_____

_____

_____

_____

_____

_____

praise

God is My Deliverer

The LORD is my light and my salvation—
whom shall I fear?
The LORD is the stronghold of my life—
of whom shall I be afraid?

PSALM 27:1

God is
My Deliverer

My Lord, forgive me for holding onto my fears. I often feel anxious for my children. I worry that they will not follow your ways. Lord, set me free from an anxious mind. Help me to trust you.

God is My Deliverer

Father, for all eternity I will sing of the security only you can provide. I rest secure in the knowledge that when you called me by name, you made me yours. No matter where the trials of my life take me, you will deliver me safely. I need not fear anything.

thanksgiving

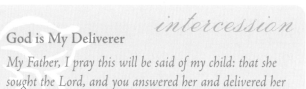

God is My Deliverer

My Father, I pray this will be said of my child: that she sought the Lord, and you answered her and delivered her from all her fears. May her face be radiant and unashamed because she looked to you for reassurance. Help her to know that your perfect love casts out fear.

God is Holy

Holy, holy, holy
* is the Lord God Almighty,*
who was, and is, and is to come.

REVELATION 4:8

_____

_____

_____

_____

_____

_____

_____

_____

_____

_____

_____

_____

_____

_____

_____

_____

_____

confession

God is Holy

Ask the Holy Spirit to search your heart and reveal anything that may be keeping you from being radiant for Jesus. If you confess and repent, see what God promises he will do:

"Blessed are the pure in heart,
    for they will see God."

MATTHEW 5:8

God is Holy

My Jesus, I love you. I rejoice greatly that you, my Jesus, were the perfect, holy sacrifice. You took my sin and in exchange poured your goodness and righteousness into me. With tears of joy I contemplate so great a love.

thanksgiving

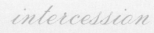

God is Holy

Dear Jesus, I pray that my child will be transformed into your likeness with ever-increasing glory, which comes from the Lord. May his heart's desire be to please you and love the things you love.

My Prayer for My Children

A Note from Fern

I would like to personally invite you to join a Moms In Touch group or start one for the mothers in your area. Women in Moms In Touch love God and their children and are committed to prayer and standing together on the promises of God's Word. As you unite with mothers in prayer, you will receive the hope that God gives and see the power of his work in the lives of your children.

To find a group in your area or to obtain information about Moms In Touch and how to start a group, please call:

1-800-949-MOMS

Fern Nichols is the mother of four children and the founder of the international organization Moms In Touch, a prayer movement that has affected thousands of women throughout the world. Since its inception, Moms In Touch groups have spread to every state and to more than 95 countries. Translated into twenty-two languages, more than 400,000 Moms In Touch International booklets have been sold. A frequent guest on Focus on the Family, Fern has also appeared on The Truth That Transforms and FAMILY LIFE Today.

Also available from Inspirio:

Prayers from a Mom's Heart
Mom's Prayers from the Heart Journal
Prayers from a Dad's Heart
Dad's Prayers from the Heart Journal
Prayers from a Grandma's Heart
Grandma's Prayers from the Heart Journal
Dad's Prayer Journal

At Inspirio we love to hear from you—
your stories, your feedback,
and your product ideas.
Please send your comments to us
by way of e-mail at
icares@zondervan.com
or to the address below:

inspirio

Attn: Inspirio Cares
5300 Patterson Avenue SE
Grand Rapids, MI 49530

If you would like further information
about Inspirio and the products we
create please visit us at:
www.inspiriogifts.com

Thank you and God bless!

...th you but some
...mixed up so do keep
...ything straightened
...enjoyed to let me
...just cannot settle
...thing, haven't even
...hay left to do a
...lonesome_ it seems
...uldn't stand it, I
...now that's foolish
...get over it but no
...heard this A.M._ the
...med storm previous
...am all through